Introduction

You may think you know your pet, but do you really? For example, do you know why your dog becomes fascinated with a particular patch of grass when you take it for a walk? Or how your cat can hear the ultrasonic squeak of a mouse? You can find the answers to these questions in *Do You Really Know Your Pet? A Pet Science Kit*, which explains how dogs and cats see, hear, taste, and much more! You'll also learn fascinating fun facts about your pet: Did you know that dogs and cats can sense an approaching storm or earthquake? Or that a cat's tail can really tell you something? With this kit, you can have fun learning and interacting with your dog or cat and truly find out what it's like to be in their world!

smell

Did You Know? Dogs have about forty times more smell receptors than humans and a sensitive nasal membrane lining that is so big, it has a surface area greater than a dog's entire body! This allows dogs to smell distinctions that our noses can't pick up. You can probably smell the difference between a hamburger and a hot dog, but your dog's nose can distinguish between an Oscar Mayer hot dog and a Ballpark frank!

Of all their senses, dogs use smell the most to learn about their environment, particularly to sniff out clues about other dogs. From sniffing a patch of grass, they can tell whether the last dog there was a friend, stranger, or enemy; what that dog had for breakfast; and even how it was feeling!

The Nose Knows

Dogs and cats can smell our moods. For instance, have you ever noticed when you're feeling sad that your dog or cat always seems to know, and will often come and cuddle with you? We give off a different scent depending on our mood or attitude.

Dogs have great scent memory—a scent can stay with a dog for life! Their scent memory is what allows them to search for missing persons, detect bombs, locate hidden drugs—and find your missing baseball glove!

smell

Did You Know? Cats have over fifteen times the number of specialized smell receptors that humans have—140 million compared to our 9 million. Like dogs, cats use their superior sense of smell to understand their surroundings. They can tell who has been in a place recently and if there is danger, and they can even detect fear in nearby people and other animals.

Smell is the first sense cats develop completely, and it is developed at birth. So even tiny kittens can smell like pros!

RECEPTORS

Smell Memory

Does your cat ever use short sniffs when it smells something? It is activating its smell memory. Cats breathe air molecules into a special chamber in the roof of their mouth called the *vomeronasal* (voh-mer-o-nay-zul) organ. There the odor is trapped, turned into an electrical signal, and transferred up to the brain, where it is stored as a smell memory forever. Dogs have a vomeronasal organ, too, which is how both can smell a person when they are just puppies or kittens and recognize that person again much later in their lives.

sound

Did You Know? Dogs can hear sounds that are up to four times farther away than sounds humans can hear. Dogs' hearing is more precise too: They can tell the difference between musical notes that are only one-eighth of a tone apart.

Study a dog with upright ears. You can see it actually tuning its ears like a satellite dish to hone in on a sound. Its seventeen ear muscles let it prick and swivel those "sound catchers" to focus on the source of the sound.

How High Can Dogs Hear?

Sound travels in waves registered in cycles per second called Hertz (Hz). Dogs can hear high-pitched sounds of up to 40,000 Hz, compared with the 20,000 Hz humans can hear. You can test this with the dog whistle. Wait until your dog is resting, then blow your dog whistle while slowly unscrewing the end. You probably cannot hear anything. But when you have found the frequency, or tone, that your dog is able to hear, you'll see it twitch its ears or lift its head.

Storm Scare
Dogs can hear tones both higher and lower than those that humans can hear. They can sense the low tones of thunder more than a hundred miles away, and some dogs will show signs of fear long before humans can even hear the thunder.

sound

Did You Know? Our human ears can't wiggle or twitch because each has only six muscles. Cats' ears have thirty different muscles, which allow them to focus on the exact location of the tiniest sound. And each ear can rotate separately!

Not only can cats focus their ears, they can also pick up on much higher sound waves than humans, and even dogs. Cats can hear sounds that travel at speeds of 65,000 Hz, and sometimes all the way up to 100,000 Hz. This allows them to hear the ultrasonic squeak of a mouse that humans can't hear and makes them great hunters, even in the dark. A kitten's hearing is especially sharp!

sight

Did You Know? What does the world look like to your dog? For one thing, it's wider. Dogs' eyes are on the sides of their heads so they have a wide field of vision. This means that dogs can see more on the sides of their heads than we can but they can't focus very well on objects that are nearby or in front of them. Humans can focus better than dogs because our eyes are close together and facing front. Because they see less space in front of them, dogs don't have good depth perception, but their sharp side vision means that they're good at guarding and at spotting prey.

Can't Eat It If It's Not Moving...

Dogs are more sensitive to light and movement than we are, but not to details. It's hard for them to see something that isn't moving. This is why a wild dog will freeze when it thinks it's been spotted by a predator.

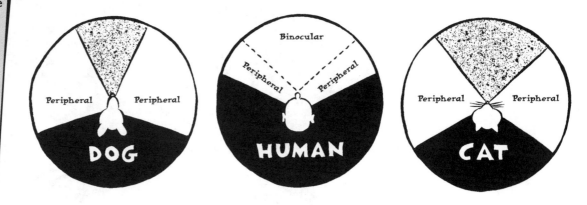

sight

Did You Know? How well can you see in the dark? Cats can see in light that is five times dimmer than the faintest light in which we can see. They can expand, or open up, their pupils to let in a lot more light than human eyes. Not only do their pupils let in more light, their eyes have fifteen layers of light-reflecting cells that help them use whatever light is available. Dogs only have one layer, and humans don't have any light-reflecting cells at all! Cats have wider fields of vision than humans, and better depth perception than humans or dogs, and they can see in the dark.

This cat's pupils are big to see in the dark!

See Like Your Pet
Try on the glasses that come with this book. Close your right eye, what do you notice? This is the way dogs see things. Next, try closing your left eye. Now you're looking at the world through a cat's eyes! Dogs and cats can't see all colors. Dogs see things in various shades of reddish gray, and cats see mostly in shades of blue and green.

To understand field of vision, and the difference between binocular and peripheral, look at the diagram on the opposite page. Here's an experiment you can do to test your own field of vision: Put your left hand directly in front of you. Looking straight ahead, see how far to the left you can move your hand before you can't see it anymore. Your dog or your cat can see much farther back than you are able.

This cat's pupils are small to let in less light for the day.

taste

Did You Know? Taste is actually the least important sense to dogs. Dogs have only seventeen hundred taste buds compared to our over nine thousand, so they can taste sweet, salty, and bitter, but not as well as we do. The smell and texture of their food is far more important to them than its taste.

Don't Forget to Chew!

As a survival instinct, dogs developed the ability to gobble their food. They have to eat their food fast before some other critter eats it—or them!

Tasty Dog Treats

Ingredients:
- 2 eggs
- 2 cups whole wheat flour
- 1 cup nonfat dry milk powder
- 1 teaspoon sugar
- 1 teaspoon salt
- 6 tablespoons margarine

1. Preheat the oven to 350 degrees Fahrenheit (176 degrees Centigrade).
2. Set aside one of the eggs. In a large bowl, mix all of the remaining ingredients with 1 cup of cold water.
3. Knead the mixture for three minutes until it forms a ball.
4. Roll out the dough on a floured surface until it is one-inch (two-and-a-half-cm) thick.
5. Cut the dough with the dog bone cookie cutter. Carefully separate your biscuits and lay them on a greased cookie sheet.
6. Whisk the remaining egg and brush it on the dough.
7. Bake in the preheated oven for 30 minutes. Be sure to have a parent help you when you're using the oven! Carefully remove the cookie sheet from the oven and let the biscuits cool before serving them to your pet. (To make extra crunchy biscuits, leave them in the oven for an hour after you turn off the heat.)

taste

Did You Know? When it comes to food, cats are pickier eaters than dogs. They tend to sniff everything before tasting it and, once the smell checks out, will delicately taste their food. Cats can taste salty, bitter, and sour but don't have taste buds that respond to sweet. Not even chocolate chip cookies! Cats are true carnivores (meat eaters), and what really makes them hungry is the smell of fat in meat.

Taste Test for Thirsty Kitties

Which flavor does your cat like best: salty, sour, bitter, or sweet? You'll need:

- 4 bowls
- plain water
- salt
- lemon, lime, or vinegar
- baking soda
- sugar

Label the bowls *salty, sour, bitter,* and *sweet.* Pour half a cup of water into each bowl. Add 1 teaspoon of salt to the salty bowl; 1 teaspoon of lemon, lime, or vinegar to the sour bowl; 1 cup of baking soda to the bitter bowl; and 1 tablespoon of sugar to the sweet bowl. Make sure they're well mixed. Mark the water levels on the outside of the bowls so you can measure how much your cat drank. Remove your cat's regular drinking water and put these four bowls out for four hours. Which water does your cat prefer?

touch

Did You Know? You like hugs don't you? Well, your dog likes to be touched as well. Praising and patting is just as important to your pet as the treat hiding in your hand.

Touch Me!

Give your dog a massage. This is a good way to give your dog some quiet affection and to learn about its body. Start at the head or the tail but don't forget the feet and legs. Gently massage its muscles and notice when they tense up and when they relax. If your dog tenses up, you may be massaging too hard or you might have found a tender spot that needs a delicate touch.

Check It Out

Dogs use their sense of touch to explore and understand their environment. They have special hairs under their jaw, on their eyebrows, and on their muzzle that help them detect air currents and an object's shape and texture.

touch

Did You Know? Whiskers give your cat the most clues about its surroundings. A cat's most sensitive touch receptors are in its whiskers. Nerve endings at the base of the whiskers send messages to the cat's brain as the whiskers sense air currents and brush past objects.

Whiskers also help your cat walk in the dark without bumping into things. By using its whiskers, a cat can tell whether it will fit through a narrow space, how big something is, and what texture it is. Cats can tell more from touching objects with their whiskers than they can by touching them with their paws, but paws still play an important role. Though not as sensitive to the touch as our hands are for us, cats' paws are used for everything from gentle grooming to fierce fighting.

Fun Feline Facts:

🐾 **The face rub:** Cats have scent glands on their chin, cheeks, and lips. That affectionate face rub is the cat transferring its scent onto you to let the world know that you belong to him or her!

🐾 A cat will knead its paws against you for various reasons. It's either saying hello and telling you it likes you, fluffing you up like a pillow for a little snooze, or it's marking you with the scent glands on its feet. In any case, you've got a happy cat on your hands!

🐾 Cats use the art of acting to scare off enemies. Even if it's shaking in its boots, a cat will stand its ground and make a show of aggression. When you see a cat's back arch and its hackles (the hair on its back) rise, the cat is trying to look bigger than it is. A cat about to attack will have dilated pupils, flattened ears, bristling whiskers, and a thumping tail. Watch out!

behaviors

Did You Know? Dogs, like their wolf cousins, instinctively travel in packs. The pack has a leader and followers. The leader is called the *alpha* dog and the second in command is called the *beta* dog. Likewise, the higher-ranking dogs are called the dominant dogs, and the lower-ranking dogs are the submissive ones. Since your family is your dog's pack, if you exhibit dominant behavior over your dog, it will take on the submissive role and be much better behaved.

Below are two lists: One suggests higher-ranking (dominant) body language, and the other suggests lower-ranking (submissive) body language. Take your dog for a walk and see what behaviors it exhibits most often when it meets another dog. Circle the characteristics that describe your dog's behavior the best.

Dominant (higher-ranking) Behaviors	Submissive (lower-ranking) Behaviors
• Puts paws, nose, or head over the other dog's shoulder • Stares and listens • Has tail up • Has ears up • Walks with stiff legs • Stands over the other animal, who lies down • Shows teeth • Rumbles and growls	• Cowers, head hunched down, shoulders down • Rolls over or lies down • Licks the other animal's mouth from below • Rubs against the other animal • Has ears down • Wags tail • Crouches • Lifts paw in a salute, reaching out (like shaking hands) • Exposes chest or stomach, rolling halfway over or jumping

behaviors

Did You Know? Although cats are often thought to be mysterious, their body language (eyes, posture, and tail) often reveals much about them.

When a cat crouches in the presence of another cat, it is a sign of submission. Rolling over can mean either one of two things, depending on the context. The action can be an invitation to play, or if your cat shows its claws and teeth, it can be a sign of aggression. When confronted by an enemy, a house cat will turn sideways and arch its back to appear larger.

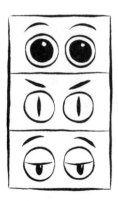

When a cat's pupils are dilated (the black center gets bigger), it means the cat is afraid.

When a cat's pupils get smaller, the cat is showing its dominance.

When a cat's eyes are half-closed, it means the cat is content.

Cat Attack

Cat games are about the thrill of the chase. Cats love to go after things just as they would tear after real prey in the wild. Toss the ball-and-string toy and observe your cat's eyes, body, and ears. What is your cat trying to tell you? What is it telling the ball?

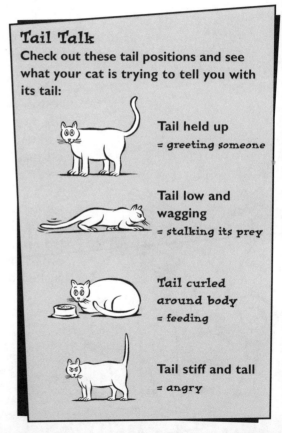

Tail Talk
Check out these tail positions and see what your cat is trying to tell you with its tail:

Tail held up
= greeting someone

Tail low and wagging
= stalking its prey

Tail curled around body
= feeding

Tail stiff and tall
= angry

pets perceive better

Dogs and cats can do amazing things with their senses of vision, hearing, smell, and touch. Sometimes their abilities go beyond anything we might imagine. And sometimes our pets surprise us with their sensitivity as well as their senses!

- "Dog Alerts Family to Heart Attack Before It Happens." "Family Pooch Senses Epileptic Seizure, Saves Boy." These kinds of headlines are not uncommon. But how does a dog know when something is about to happen? The nose knows. Dogs can pick up on the odor a person gives off just before having a heart attack, epileptic seizure, or other forms of medical emergencies.

- Other pets seem to know when to alert others that something is really wrong. Holly, a golden retriever in Seattle, once stayed by the side of the grandfather of the family for three hours after he fell down the stairs and broke his hip while in the house alone. When the family returned, she rushed to the door and led them to him.

pets perceive better

- Dogs and cats have amazing homing abilities. Both animals have been known to travel hundreds, even thousands, of miles to get back to their homes. Take the case of the Reeds, who moved from Massachusetts to Maine. Every summer after the move, their dog, Chester, would run away and find his way back to their old house in Massachusetts! This isn't that uncommon. Scientists think that this homing ability might have something to do with the sensitivity of animals to the earth's magnetism. Think of how birds, whales, and other animals who migrate are able to find their way back to their same nesting and breeding grounds year after year.

other fun fascinating facts

- Would you believe big dogs eat less than little dogs? Pound for pound, big guys scarf up fewer calories than little ankle biters.

- How do cats always land on their feet? Cats have 244 bones. We only have 204. Some think the extra bones, greater muscular control, and a sensitive inner ear allow your cat to land on its feet. Their advanced inner ear gives them perfect balance and the ability to orient themselves instantly.

- More than half the dogs in America know at least one trick. What is your dog's specialty?

- Cats can stare for hours without blinking. You'd think they'd get bored!

- Dogs don't have sweat glands, so when they get hot, they pant to release body heat from their mouths. Cats sweat, but most don't do it from their skin—they sweat from their feet.

- Cats' foot bones have evolved so they permanently walk and run on their toes. Cats can climb up almost anything, but the shape of their claws makes it a lot harder for them to climb down. When stuck (in a tree, for example), they will awkwardly back down, jump down, or cry for help.

- Dogs can get sunburned. To keep your dog's skin from turning pink in the sun, douse it in sunscreen (the human kind is fine). This will prevent a bad burn.